THIS BOOK BELONGS TO

Manufactured by Amazon.ca
Acheson, AB

30002066R00061